Mightiest Rivers

Myra Junyk

Series Editor
Jeffrey D. Wilhelm

Much thought, debate, and research went into choosing and ranking the 10 items in each book in this series. We realize that everyone has his or her own opinion of what is most significant, revolutionary, amazing, deadly, and so on. As you read, you may agree with our choices, or you may be surprised — and that's the way it should be!

an imprint of

SCHOLASTIC

www.scholastic.com/librarypublishing

A Rubicon book published in association with Scholastic Inc.

Rubicon © 2008 Rubicon Publishing Inc.
www.rubiconpublishing.com

 is a trademark of The 10 Books

Associate Publishers: Kim Koh, Miriam Bardswich
Project Editor: Amy Land
Editor: Jessica Calleja
Creative Director: Jennifer Drew
Project Manager/Designer: Jeanette MacLean
Graphic Designer: Brandon Köpke

The publisher gratefully acknowledges the following for permission to reprint copyrighted material in this book.

Every reasonable effort has been made to trace the owners of copyrighted material and to make due acknowledgment. Any errors or omissions drawn to our attention will be gladly rectified in future editions.

"Speaking Out," excerpt from "Doing it for Themselves," *Bangkok Post* Story: Sanitsuda Ekachai.

Cover: Tributary of the Mackenzie River–© Michael T. Sedam/CORBIS

Library and Archives Canada Cataloguing in Publication

Junyk, Myra
  The 10 mightiest rivers / Myra Junyk.

Includes index.
ISBN 978-1-55448-519-2

    1. Readers (Elementary). 2. Readers—Rivers. I. Title.
II. Title: Ten mightiest rivers.

PE1117.J9613 2007a   428.6   C2007-906700-X

1 2 3 4 5 6 7 8 9 10   10   17 16 15 14 13 12 11 10 09 08

Printed in Singapore

Contents

GO WITH THE FLOW...

Mightiest rivers? You may think the two words don't belong together. But if you think about it, rivers are mighty important to human beings. They provide water for drinking and irrigation. They have helped to shape human history as people have flocked to their banks, developing settlements that have grown into cities. They are an important means of transport. And they are a valuable source of energy.

Need any more reasons why rivers are mighty? Well, some rivers are so beautiful they have inspired great works of art, music, and writing! And almost all rivers have helped to shape the landscape, carving their way through the land over millions of years.

Rivers can also be extremely destructive — when they flood over, they can wipe out towns and villages, killing thousands. On the flip side, natural flooding cycles build up fertile soil, which can be beneficial to farming and agriculture.

One sad fact is that many of the world's largest rivers have been so mistreated by human beings that today they are more like sewers full of human and industrial wastes than bodies of water. Out of the 10 rivers on our list, only one has not been touched by pollution!

In this book, we present what we think are the 10 mightiest rivers in the world. We ranked them based on their length and the area they cover; their importance to the life, agriculture, and economy of the areas through which they flow; their role in shaping the history of the region; and the legends or works of art they have inspired.

IF YOU HAD TO NAME THE MIGHTIEST RIVER IN THE WORLD, WHICH ONE WOULD YOU CHOOSE?

The Murray is fed by several rivers as it journeys from its source in the Australian Alps. The main rivers that feed into it are the Darling and the Murrumbidgee.

ER

LENGTH: About 1,550 mi.

CONTINENT: Australia

WHY SO MIGHTY? Australians in three states depend on it for their livelihood!

Australia's Aboriginal people believe that millions of years ago, Ngurunderi, their all-powerful ancestor, went on a journey through Australia. Legend has it that during this journey Ngurunderi began chasing a large fish. He pursued the fish on a raft while launching spears at it. But the fish swam a weaving path, carving out the river and its tributaries as it went. It was this chase between hunter and prey that was responsible for the creation of the mighty Murray River.

Today, the Murray River and its basin are a lifeline for Australia's environment and economy. Millions of Australians, in cities and in rural areas, depend on the river for their drinking water, agriculture, and recreation. The Murray is especially important to farmers because it is the main source of water for crop irrigation.

Over the years, pollution and drought have created challenges for the Murray. Water is polluted, wetlands are drying up, fish and wildlife are struggling to survive, and the soil in many areas is becoming too salty for plants to grow. The government and concerned citizens recognize that protective steps must be taken. It is a huge job to make sure that people are able to earn a living from using the basin, while still protecting the river and the natural habitat of the many birds, animals, and fish that make the area their home.

---

tributaries: *smaller rivers or streams that flow into a larger river*
basin: *area of land that is drained by a river system*
irrigation: *method of supplying water to crops*
wetlands: *areas such as marshes that are mostly covered by shallow water*

MURRAY RIVER

? The Murray River Basin covers one-seventh of Australia's total area. What does this tell you about its importance?

WHERE IN THE WORLD?

N W E S

AUSTRALIA

NORTHERN TERRITORY

QUEENSLAND

WESTERN AUSTRALIA

SOUTH AUSTRALIA

NEW SOUTH WALES

Murrumbridge River — Canberra

INDIAN OCEAN

VICTORIA

TASMANIA

There are over 10,000 known sites of native people in the Murray-Darling Basin.

Quick Fact

A river basin drains all of the land around a major river. Basins can be divided into watersheds. Within each watershed, all water runs to the lowest point — a stream, river, lake, or ocean. On its way, water travels over the surface of the land or it seeps into the soil and travels as groundwater.

MOMENT IN TIME

The first European settlers to discover this mighty waterway were Hamilton Human and William Hovell in 1824. They were sent to find new grazing land and to also find an answer to the mystery of where New South Wales's western rivers flowed to. Several years later, in 1830, Captain Charles Sturt navigated down the river and named it after Sir George Murray, a soldier and politician. After Sturt's discovery, the Murray River became a major trade route as steamboats traveled up and down the length of the river, transporting produce from riverside towns and cities.

LIFE ON THE RIVER

The Murray River is the major water source for over 1.5 million households. Seventy-five percent of the water used for farming in Australia comes from the Murray and the smaller rivers that flow into it. The river system drains most of inland Victoria, New South Wales, and southern Queensland, totaling one-seventh of Australia's landmass. The main crops grown in the region include barley, oats, wheat, fruits, vegetables, and cotton. The Murray River Basin is full of wildlife, although quite a few of its native fish, such as the Murray cod, trout cod, and golden perch, are endangered. The basin also has 30,000 wetlands, which are breeding grounds for birds from Japan and China.

? Research some of the endangered birds and animals of the Murray River Basin — and the reasons why they are facing extinction.

Quick Fact

Aboriginals have lived along the Murray for 30,000 years. Various groups included Ingalta, Moorundie, Goodwarra, Parrian-Kaperre, Tongwillum, and Yoorlooarra. The Ngarrindjeri people lived along the Murray and the Coorong and are South Australia's largest Aboriginal community.

10

9 8 7 6

Fantastic Voyage

Leanne Jarchow

Leanne Jarchow is the first to admit that she's not a serious athlete. Amazingly though, this grandmother paddled the entire length of the Murray River in 41 days! This photo essay shows some of the things that caught her attention.

"The noise from the animals and birds was fantastic as you paddled through," Jarchow said. "Magic."

The journey changed Jarchow's feelings about the Murray. She realized how much both humans and animals depend on the river.

Jarchow also saw a disturbing sight on the river — floating scum from pollution.

This tawny frogmouth bird sits very still by the river and disguises itself to look like a tree stump.

The Expert Says...

" The great River Murray has its own peculiarities and its grandeur and beauty of scenery. It is estimated that with its tributaries it drains half the continent. "

— Leila Pirani, author of *The Old Man River of Australia*

Take Note

The Murray River stands at #10 on our list. This mighty river has been important to Australian Aboriginals for thousands of years. Today it continues to support agriculture and the economy of a major section of the country.
- How do you think the condition of the Murray River and its basin will affect the people, animals, and environment of Australia? What do you think will happen if it gets worse?

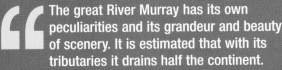

5   4   3   2   1

Up until 70 years ago, hunters and Native peoples were the only ones who lived in the Mackenzie River Valley.

MACKENZIE RIVER DELTA—© LOWELL GEORGIA/CORBIS

RIVER

LENGTH: About 1,120 mi.

CONTINENT: North America

WHY SO MIGHTY? The Mackenzie is one of the world's last untouched rivers. It is full of natural resources and is home to a variety of wildlife.

The Dene people of the Arctic call it "Deh Cho," which means "Big River." This name definitely fits because the Mackenzie-Peace-Finlay system is the second-largest river system in North America, after the Mississippi's. Like a gentle giant, it rules calmly over the waterways of the great northwest.

While the Mackenzie River Basin is home to many birds and animals, it is lightly populated by humans, with only about 10,000 inhabitants. Although it can be traveled from one end to the other, the river is only navigable for five months of the year because it freezes over in the winter.

In the 1970s, oil and gas were discovered under the Mackenzie River. Energy companies wanted to build a pipeline through the river valley, but Native peoples thought this would spoil the area's natural environment. The peoples quickly put a stop to the pipeline plan. The death of the pipeline plan put an end to oil exploration on the Mackenzie. This has left the river practically untouched to this day.

In recent years, Native groups have been rethinking about building the pipeline. How much longer will the Mackenzie be one of the most undeveloped, lightly populated, and purest river valleys in the world?

navigable: *allowing ships to travel through*

MACKENZIE RIVER

An inukshuk is a stone landmark that helps to guide Inuit across the treeless tundra of the Canadian Arctic.

MOMENT IN TIME

While working as a fur trapper in the province of Alberta, Canada, Alexander Mackenzie heard rumors from local Native peoples about a direct water route to the Pacific Ocean. In 1789, Mackenzie set off with eight men in three canoes to uncover this mysterious route. On their journey, they did not find a direct route to the Pacific, but instead discovered another broad river that headed north of the Rocky Mountains. They followed this river for 40 days until they hit the Arctic Ocean. This broad river eventually became known as the "Mackenzie," named after the courageous fur trader who discovered it.

Shortly after the river was discovered by Alexander Mackenzie, many fur trading posts were set up along its banks.

WHERE IN THE WORLD?

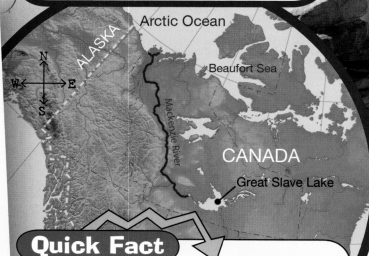

Arctic Ocean

ALASKA

Beaufort Sea

Mackenzie River

CANADA

Great Slave Lake

Quick Fact

People who live on the Mackenzie River get their sense of direction from the river itself, which flows downstream to the north. They talk about "going up south" and "going down north."

LIFE ON THE RIVER

Many different people live around the Mackenzie River, both non-Native and Native groups, including the Dene, Métis, and Inuit. The river is important to these people because it serves as a transportation route to the western Arctic. Because it is navigable only five months of the year, these communities depend on the barges that travel along the river during the short summer season.

The Mackenzie River Valley is also home to migrating snow geese and tundra swans. Beluga whales are found in the waters near the delta area.

---

delta: *triangular-shaped deposit of soil at the mouth of a river*

Quick Fact

The clay soil of the Mackenzie River Valley would support agriculture, but the cold climate prevents farming.

A pipeline would disturb the movement of caribou that live in the region because building would interfere with their migration.

TO BUILD OR NOT TO BUILD?

The debate rages on about the Mackenzie Valley Pipeline. Building of the pipeline would affect the river, its inhabitants, and the surrounding environment in many ways. Take a look at this comparison chart to get both sides of the story.

PROS

🔥 Natural gas found along the Mackenzie would replace coal as a power source. Coal is the dirtiest of fossil fuels, while natural gas is the cleanest.

🔥 The pipeline would boost the economy of the north by creating jobs.

🔥 The pipeline would support the province of Alberta's oil mining industry by supplying gas, which would act as a second energy source to make up for shrinking energy supplies.

CONS

🔥 Building of the pipeline would damage one of the planet's last untouched areas of wilderness.

🔥 The clean gas delivered by the pipeline would be used as an energy source to support Alberta's oil mining industry. This oil will be used to fuel cars, which create gases like carbon dioxide that pollute the environment.

🔥 New roads, airports, bases, and towns would be built as a result. This would disrupt the people living in the area as well as an environment that is home to many animals.

The Expert Says...

❝ [W]e believe it's [the pipeline project's] not a question of 'if' but rather 'when.' ❞

— Bob German, CFO of Horizon North Logistics Inc.

? The Mackenzie River's thinly populated basin is one of the last great unspoiled areas of the world. Why do you think it's important to preserve the natural condition of this river?

Take Note

The Mackenzie River is Canada's longest river. Unlike the Murray River, it is unspoiled by pollution and industry. It flows in at #9.
• Do you think the Native groups should stop the pipeline plan or move it forward? Explain your answer.

5   4   3   2   1

The Danube is very popular with tourists. Many cruises are offered along this famous river.

LENGTH: About 1,770 mi.

CONTINENT: Europe

WHY SO MIGHTY? Western Europe's most important river also has a romantic history that has inspired generations.

The Danube has been an important international waterway for centuries. Known in history as one of the long-standing frontiers of the Roman Empire, the river flows through 10 countries. Palaces, cathedrals, old-world villages, and majestic cities tell the tale of its colorful past.

Countries with centuries of history and cultural richness line the banks of this fairy-tale river. Called the "queen of Europe's rivers," the Danube is wrapped in myths and legends. No other river in the world has inspired so many poets, musicians, and painters to create masterpieces.

But the Danube isn't just an inspiration for artists. It is a major transportation route, commercial link, and producer of hydroelectric power. Sadly, like the Murray, years of misuse have put the Danube in danger. Countries lining this mighty waterway are now scrambling for ways to undo this damage before it's too late.

hydroelectric: *relating to energy created by falling or moving water*

DANUBE RIVER

WHERE IN THE WORLD?

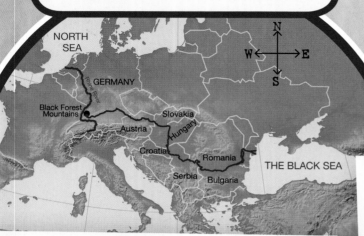

NORTH SEA

GERMANY

Rhine River

Black Forest Mountains

Slovakia

Austria

Hungary

Croatia

Serbia

Romania

Bulgaria

THE BLACK SEA

N W E S

Quick Fact

The Danube is a source of drinking water to about 10 million people. But raw sewage, chemicals, waste, and oil have been draining into it. This is creating serious water pollution problems that are affecting the quality of drinking water.

Think about where your drinking water comes from. How would you feel if the source of your water was being polluted like the Danube? What could you do to try and stop this from happening?

MOMENT IN TIME

At the height of the Roman Empire, the Danube served as its northern border. It later became an invasion route for those who wanted to take over the empire. Roman strongholds along its shores were settlements that later became the modern cities of Vienna, Budapest, and Belgrade.

strongholds: *heavily armed defensive structures*

LIFE ON THE RIVER

The Danube supports central Europe's agriculture and industry. Cargo ships transport chemicals, iron ore, coal, grain, and steel. Since the Danube is connected by a canal to the Rhine River, barges are able to travel all the way from the Black Sea to the North Sea by water. Dams have made it a major source of hydroelectric power.

Unfortunately, flooding and pollution threaten the river's natural habitats. Fish populations have suffered, although many species such as pike, sturgeon, eel, and herring are still found in the Danube Delta. The delta is also a nature preserve for birds like the white-tailed sea eagle, the dalmatian pelican, and the black stork.

Cargo ships use the Danube as a route for moving goods through Europe.

ALL IMAGES–SHUTTERSTOCK,ISTOCKPHOTO

10   9   **8**   7   6

THE BLUE DANUBE WALTZ

This report explains how the Danube River inspired one of the world's most popular compositions.

Most people who live in Europe think of the Danube as the *blue* Danube, yet this couldn't be further from the truth. Over time, the Danube has been gray, faintly green, and now with all of the pollution, a muddy brown — but never blue! Part of this misunderstanding comes from the famous "Blue Danube," a waltz written by composer Johann Strauss in 1867.

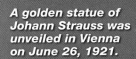

A golden statue of Johann Strauss was unveiled in Vienna on June 26, 1921.

So what is the story behind this famous piece of music? This well-known waltz was composed in Vienna in the 19th century. It has now become almost a second national anthem to Austria and is a reminder of the Danube River's great historical importance. The river's twists and turns are a reminder of the ups and downs of Austria's history.

"The Blue Danube" was first performed in concert on February 9, 1867. Even though it wasn't very popular at first, it has since become one of the most loved pieces of classical music. It has also created a romantic myth surrounding the Danube, making it one of Europe's most popular tourist attractions.

 Think of a song that you can easily identify with. How does the song make you feel?

The Expert Says...

"We have to learn to live together with the river again ... a lot of villages and infrastructure were built in places where the water circulation of the region cannot tolerate it in the longer term."

— Gabor Ungvari, environmental economist

infrastructure: *human-made systems built to support urban development*

Take Note

The Danube River waltzes into the #8 spot. In addition to being an important waterway, it has played a significant role in shaping Europe's history, culture, and economy.
• Go online and find out about some of the most popular tourist sites along the Danube. Would you choose a cruise down this river for a vacation? Why or why not?

5   4   3   2   1

In Vietnam, some people live in boats on the Mekong River. The canals are their streets!

LENGTH: About 3,045 mi.

CONTINENT: Asia

WHY SO MIGHTY? The Mekong is the main water source for over 60 million people.

Today, one in every three people in Laos, Thailand, Cambodia, and Vietnam live in the Lower Mekong River Basin. In countless ways, the lives of many people are linked together through the river's history of war, colonialism, and modernization.

The Mekong may not be the longest river on our list, but it has one of the most diverse ecosystems in the world. It also gives over 60 million people water for power, transportation, and fishing. A few of the countries lining its shores want to build 50 dams along the Mekong to supply power. If these plans are carried out, the undisturbed Mekong River system will drastically change.

This is because millions of people, animals, and plants depend on the basin's yearly flood cycle for their living. Dams could damage the Mekong River system on a large scale. The water cycle would change, areas would be flooded, fisheries would be damaged, endangered wildlife habitats would be destroyed, farmland would receive less water, and an estimated 100,000 people would be forced to move.

---

colonialism: *policy of one country bringing control or influence over another*
ecosystems: *communities of animals, plants, and bacteria, plus the environment where they live*

MEKONG RIVER

WHERE IN THE WORLD?

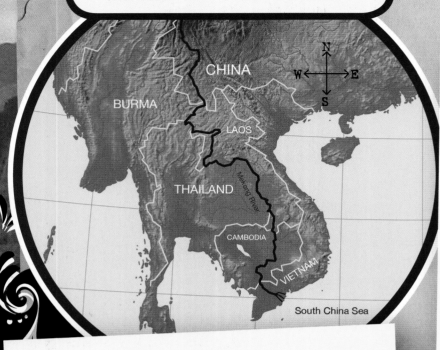

CHINA
BURMA
LAOS
THAILAND
Mekong River
CAMBODIA
VIETNAM
South China Sea

N
W E
S

Quick Fact

Because of rapids and sandbars, ships can only sail about 350 miles up the Mekong River.

LIFE ON THE RIVER

Over 60 million people live in the Mekong River Basin. Many earn a living by farming or fishing. The major crop is rice, but pineapples, sugarcane, and peanuts are also grown. Because of irrigation from the Mekong, farmers can grow three to four crops a year.

The river is like a supermarket. Every morning, thousands of people gather along its banks to buy and sell goods!

? Local communities use the seasonal pattern of floods to plan their planting and harvesting of crops. Why is this important?

MOMENT IN TIME

The first European exploration was called the French Mekong Expedition. It was led by Ernest Doudard de Lagrée and Francis Garnier and lasted from 1866 to 1868. They discovered that the Mekong has too many falls and rapids to be a useful travel route. During their harsh journey, the explorers suffered from fever and dysentery. They also had wounds caused by leeches. These wounds became infected because the explorers were forced to walk barefoot once they had worn out their supply of shoes.

dysentery: *infection that causes severe diarrhea*

The Expert Says...

"Many of those who live in poverty are very closely dependent on the resources of the Mekong River and the Mekong River Basin, which means that if development is to proceed without care, there's potential to [ease] poverty, but also to exacerbate it."

— Philip Hirsch, Associate Professor of Sydney University

exacerbate: *worsen; aggravate*

SPEAKING OUT!

Dams and pollution have already had a negative effect on the Mekong River by disrupting natural flood cycles, flooding farmers' lands, destroying fish habitats, and killing plants. A group of villagers, whose families have called the Mekong home for centuries, are speaking out against more developments. Here are their quotes …

" We fishermen have knowledge about the Mekong based on our time-tested experiences … But policy-makers dismiss us as simple folk so that they can dismiss our voices and impose their policies, which only benefit businessmen but destroy our way of life. "

— Oon Thammawong, fisherman

" Before, we never ran out of food, thanks to the Mekong. Since we were children, we've been using its clean, clear water for drinking, bathing, and whatnot. But now the river has become murky and dirty …" "

— Gaewsai Saoleesang, villager

" Chiang Khong is bombarded with mega-projects [dams] … But the worst is yet to come … "

— Somkiat Kuenchiangsa, environmentalist

" Destroy the rapids and you destroy the Mekong and the villagers' ways of life … We can't discount the heavy use of farm chemicals as one of the sources of pollution in the Mekong … "

— Rian Jinnarat, community leader

? Why do you think it's important to listen to local people who actually live and work on the Mekong River, as well as businesses that are encouraging development?

Take Note

As Southeast Asia's most important river, the Mekong rolls in at #7. It has provided for the people of four countries for centuries.

• Like many rivers in this book, the Mekong is negatively affected by pollution, overuse, and interference with the river's natural flow. Research what is being done by the government, businesses, and people to improve the situation.

ALL IMAGES–SHUTTERSTOCK.ISTOCKPHOTO

5   4   3   2   1

6 MISSISSIPPI

Almost all of the water between the Appalachian Mountains and the Rockies flows through the Mississippi or its tributaries.

RIVER

LENGTH: About 2,300 mi.

CONTINENT: North America

WHY SO MIGHTY? Starting in Minnesota and ending in the Gulf of Mexico, the Mississippi River is a major trade highway in the United States.

Old Man River, Great River, Big Muddy, Father of the Waters — these are just a few of the many nicknames the mighty Mississippi has been given over the years. Of all the rivers on our list, the Mississippi's history is definitely one of the most mysterious and colorful. Out of its swampy waters springs a living landscape of music and legend.

The Mississippi drains half of North America. Its river basin is larger than Great Britain, France, Ireland, Spain, Portugal, Germany, Austria, Italy, Greece, and Turkey put together. Its fertile valley has been home to humans for more than 10,000 years. Native Americans built great cities along its banks and traveled its waters to trade with other tribes. In 1541, Hernando de Soto was the first European to glimpse the great river. He was even buried on its shores.

The Mississippi is a very important part of American life. It is a major highway for transporting farm and industrial goods. Over the years, the river has made its mark on the country's geography, environment, economy, and even literature.

Because much of the land along the Mississippi is low-lying, it uses the world's biggest levee system to control its water flow. But in 2005, Hurricane Katrina destroyed many of the levees in New Orleans and caused devastating damage that is going to affect the Mississippi's environment and people for years to come.

---

levee: *small wall built to protect populated areas from overflowing bodies of water*

MISSISSIPPI RIVER

WHERE IN THE WORLD?

CANADA

Lake Itaska

Minneapolis

Wisconsin

Minnesota

Iowa

U.S.A.

Illinois

Missouri

Kentucky

Arkansas

Tennessee

Mississippi

Louisiana

Baton Rouge

Gulf of Mexico

MOMENT IN TIME

The Mississippi River became a part of the United States when Louisiana was bought from France in 1803. It later played an important role in the outcome of the American Civil War when the Union and the Confederacy were fighting for control of the river. The Union victory at the Battle of Vicksburg in 1863 was a turning point that led to their final victory in the Civil War. This victory gave the Union control of the lower Mississippi River.

Quick Fact

Native peoples have lived along the Mississippi since 9000 B.C. The river and its tributaries were an important trade route. One of the largest settlements was located near present-day St. Louis, Missouri, where as many as 20,000 people made their homes almost 2,000 years ago. By the time European exploration began, these settlements were only a memory. It is believed that smallpox was unknowingly brought over from Europe and wiped out most of the Native American villages.

LIFE ON THE RIVER

Today, the Mississippi River is one of the greatest commercial waterways of the world. Locks and dams help control water flow and provide reliable transportation. Barges and other vessels travel up and down this great river. Ocean vessels can sail up to Baton Rouge, Louisiana, while smaller boats can travel as far as Minneapolis.

locks: *series of enclosed areas where boats are raised or lowered*

Quick Fact

Writer Mark Twain wrote a book called the *Adventures of Huckleberry Finn*. Based in the mid-1800s before the Civil War, it is about the friendship that grows between a boy named Huckleberry Finn and a runaway enslaved African named Jim as they flee south on the Mississippi River.

In the 1800s, steamboats sailed the Mississippi carrying cowboys, gamblers, and French and English settlers to the American West. This French influence is still felt in the delta area.

Adventures of HUCKLEBERRY FINN. (Tom Sawyer's Comrade) BY MARK TWAIN. ILLUSTRATED.

Cover from the original edition of Huckleberry Finn from 1885

Starting from Scratch

This report explains how nature can pack a powerful punch.

New Orleans is bordered by water. Because it rests almost seven feet below sea level, the city's safety depends on one of the world's biggest levee systems. But when Hurricane Katrina hit on August 29, 2005, the system could not withstand such a strong storm. Levees along the Mississippi River Gulf Outlet broke in about 20 places, flooding much of the area.

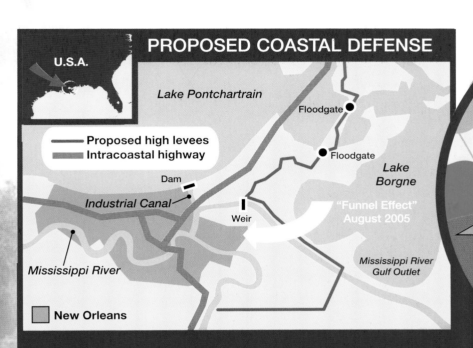

PROPOSED COASTAL DEFENSE

U.S.A.

Lake Pontchartrain

Floodgate

— Proposed high levees
— Intracoastal highway

Floodgate

Dam

Lake Borgne

Industrial Canal

Weir

"Funnel Effect" August 2005

Mississippi River

Mississippi River Gulf Outlet

New Orleans

IMPROVED LEVEE DESIGN

28 ft.

To stop this from happening again, engineers want to:

- build a system of high levees to the east and north of New Orleans. These would be wider and higher than those found in the city center.

- build weirs into the Mississippi River Gulf Outlet to control water flow and dam the mouth of the Industrial Canal.

- set up floating barge dams with built-in pumps to drive back storm flows.

weirs: *low dams built across a river or stream to raise its level or change its flow*

Many people lost their homes, loved ones, and even their lives because of the floods caused by Hurricane Katrina. Why do you think people would want to move back to this area even after such a devastating natural disaster?

The Expert Says...

" The river system formed pathways for much of the settlement of the central United States. The advent of the steamboat in 1812 brought dependable transportation ... "

— Stanley W. Trimble, assistant professor of Geography, University of California, Los Angeles

advent: *arrival*

Take Note

As North America's longest river, with a basin covering an area larger than many countries put together, the mighty Mississippi sweeps into the #6 spot. It has a fascinating history and has inspired more legends, books, and music than even the Danube.

- Even though humans build structures to try to control the environment, Hurricane Katrina proved how uncontrollable nature can be. Does this natural disaster make the Mississippi seem more or less of a mighty river? Explain your answer.

2   1

Hindus regard the Ganges as a holy river — they bathe in it so their sins will be forgiven.

LENGTH: About 1,550 mi.

CONTINENT: Asia

WHY SO MIGHTY? Beginning in the Himalayan Mountains, the Ganges is India's most important river. It is considered holy by Hindus around the world.

According to Hindu mythology, Ganga is the goddess of the River Ganges. Long ago, Ganga fell to Earth to help a king whose ancestors had been burned to ashes. Only the cleansing waters of the Ganges could free the ancestors from the ashes to live in peace. Since then, most Hindus believe that if the ashes of their dead are placed in the river, they will be given a smooth transition to the next life. Hindus also believe that bathing in the river will wash away their sins.

Twisting across northern India, the Ganges is not just a sacred river to the Hindus, but also a sacred being. For centuries it has been called "Ganga Ma" or "Mother Ganges." Every year about one million Hindus come from all parts of India to bathe in the waters of this river.

While the Ganges is an important holy symbol, it is also a vital source of water for the people who live on its banks. But its condition has worsened as India's population and industries continue to grow. Pollution has become especially serious in the last few years. Bathing in the river and drinking its water are now dangerous. This is creating a huge problem for the 300 million people who rely on the river's water for day-to-day survival, mainly because the biggest killer in India is water-borne diseases. Now the challenge is to clean up this river, so that it can be enjoyed by generations to come.

GANGES RIVER

WHERE IN THE WORLD?

CHINA

HIMALAYAN MOUNTAINS

Ganges River

NEPAL

BHUTAN

INDIA

BANGLADESH

INDIA

BURMA

Calcutta

Bay of Bengal

Quick Fact

During monsoon season, rains cause flooding in low-lying delta areas. At least 20% of Bangladesh is flooded every year.

monsoon: *wind pattern that reverses direction with the seasons*

People in Bangladesh build their houses on stilts so they won't get washed away by the yearly floods. What else do you think people can do to avoid damage from floods? Make a list.

The Bengal tiger lives in the Ganges Delta.

MOMENT IN TIME

Completed in 1974, a dam was built about six miles from the Indian side of the border between India and Bangladesh. India uses the dam to control the flow of the Ganges. It redirects the Ganges River water into a distributary, the Hooghly River, during the dry season. It also flushes out silt that has been building up at the major port of Calcutta on the Hooghly River. Bangladesh and India have had many debates about how the dam cuts off Bangladesh's water supply. Also in Bangladesh, the redirection of water has raised salt levels, contaminated fisheries, hindered navigation, and posed a threat to water quality and public health. This feud was not settled until 1996, when the two countries agreed to share the water equally.

LIFE ON THE RIVER

The Ganges is the main water source for the people who live along its banks. It gives them water for cooking, farming, drinking, and washing. The floodplain is especially important for farming in India and Bangladesh. Crops that are grown on the floodplain include rice, potatoes, wheat, sugarcane, mustard, and sesame.

The mangrove swamps in the Ganges Delta provide a habitat for many unique plants and animals, including the Royal Bengal tiger.

distributary: *branch of a river that flows away from the main stream*

floodplain: *low, flat area of land along the course of a river that is likely to be flooded*

The Expert Says...

"The Ganges Basin is India's most extensive, most agriculturally productive, and most densely populated region."

— Ashok K. Dutt, professor of Geography and Regional Planning, University of Akron, Ohio

10   9   8   7   6

Cleaning Up the Ganges

Over the years, many campaigns and much effort have gone into cleaning up the Ganges, as described in this report.

PROBLEM

Pollution is the greatest threat to the Ganges River. Gallons of waste flow into the Ganges every day. Most of this waste comes from sewage, trash, food, and human and animal remains. This is causing water-borne diseases diseases, such as diarrhea, cholera, and typhoid.

Thousands of dead bodies are cremated and placed in the river every year. This ancient spiritual practice is contributing to the pollution problem. In addition, thousands of animal carcasses (mainly cattle) are left along its banks every year.

Many industries are also releasing dangerous chemicals into the Ganges. As recently as 2004, the WHO reported that an estimated 1.1 million liters (290,000 gallons) of raw sewage is dumped into the Ganges every minute. Runoff from farms in the Ganges Basin adds chemical fertilizers and pesticides. The construction of dams is redirecting water and adding to the pollution crisis.

cremated: *burned and reduced to ashes*

ACTION

The Campaign for a Clean Ganges is one of the first environmental efforts in India. In 1992, the campaign introduced a program that included a sewage treatment plan. The sewage would be stored in ponds that use bacteria and algae to break down waste and clean the water.

In 2002, another program was launched to raise national awareness, help local communities take charge of the problem, and help businesses and local governments build relationships. In 2003, this program organized the first national Clean Ganga Day. Several have been held every year since.

algae: *simple, rootless plants that grow in bodies of water*

 How do you think pollution is going to affect the Ganges River, its people, and its habitat in years to come? Why do you think it's so important to fix this problem now, before it gets any worse?

There are about 30 cities, 70 towns, and thousands of villages along the banks of the Ganges. Nearly all of the sewage from these population centers passes directly into the river.

Quick Fact

The Ganges River dolphin is one of four species of river dolphins in the world! The dolphin is now threatened. Its greatest danger is habitat changes caused by the building of dams. Pollution and fishing are also considered serious threats.

Take Note

Flowing in at #5, the Ganges stands out from the other rivers on our list because while it does have agricultural and economic importance, its unique claim to fame is its spiritual and religious status.
• Does the Ganges River's symbolic importance make you feel differently about how mighty rivers should be judged? Explain.

5   4   3   2   1

4 CONGO RIVER

The Congo River is about 10 miles wide in some places. During periods of high rainfall, the Congo carries more water than any other river on earth except the Amazon.

LENGTH: About 2,670 mi.

CONTINENT: Africa

WHY SO MIGHTY? As the central waterway in Africa, the Congo River Basin and the surrounding forests support millions of people and are home to millions of unique plants and animals.

Deep in the heart of Africa flows the Congo River. The river and the rain forest it passes through have attracted many explorers. In 1816, James Kingston Tuckey, a captain in the British Royal Navy, went on an expedition to discover the source of the Congo River. It was the first time a European explorer ventured into the inner regions of the Congo. His attempt proved to be disastrous. The captain and his crew faced overwhelming obstacles — the powerful river rapids and yellow fever, a dangerous disease spread by mosquitoes. But even though Tuckey failed, his journey sparked interest in other Europeans who ventured out to unlock the mystery of the Congo River.

Though the Congo River is important to the area's economy, agriculture, and environment, it has an unsettled past and even more uncertain future. Recent problems of poaching, deforestation, and pollution are threatening the health of the Congo River Basin. As forests are shrinking, wildlife is disappearing. But one business keeps booming — logging. All of these factors are putting the environment, wildlife, local people, and economy at risk.

poaching: *illegal trapping and killing of animals*

CONGO RIVER

MOMENT IN TIME

In 1866, British explorer David Livingstone set off for central Africa to find the source of the Nile River. After a few years without hearing from Livingstone, Henry Morton Stanley was sent to find him. After finding Livingstone in 1871, Stanley returned to England a hero. Then he set out for Africa once again. He explored central Africa and traveled down the length of the Lualaba and Congo Rivers, reaching the Atlantic Ocean in 1877. In 1879, supported by King Leopold II of Belgium, Stanley returned to Africa where he opened the lower Congo to commerce by the construction of roads. This turned out to be devastating for the Congo region because it led to the claiming of African territories. Leopold's officer exploited the local people by forcing them to do manual labor without pay and killed thousands who would not cooperate.

LIFE ON THE RIVER

Passing through the world's second-largest rain forest, the Congo River Basin is full of unique plants and animals. People who live along the river use its water for drinking, farming, and washing. Its fish are also a major source of food for the entire area. Although some parts of the river cannot be traveled because of rapids and waterfalls, the river is still the main route for much of Africa's trade. Cotton, sugar, coffee, and copper are moved using steamboats. The Congo is potentially Africa's greatest source of hydroelectric power, especially along Livingstone Falls.

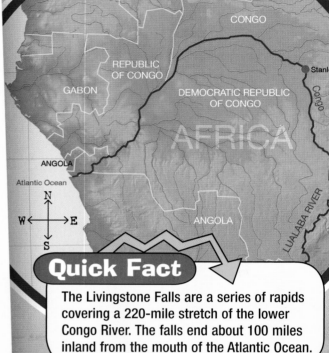

CONGO
REPUBLIC OF CONGO
GABON
DEMOCRATIC REPUBLIC OF CONGO
Stanley Falls
AFRICA
Congo
ANGOLA
Atlantic Ocean
N W E S
ANGOLA
LUALABA RIVER

Quick Fact

The Livingstone Falls are a series of rapids covering a 220-mile stretch of the lower Congo River. The falls end about 100 miles inland from the mouth of the Atlantic Ocean.

Quick Fact

Half of the world's mountain gorillas live in the Congo region. Fewer than 600 are left in the world because of poaching and war. The president of the Democratic Republic of Congo, Joseph Kabila, has promised to help protect these endangered animals.

The African rain forest is home to the tribes of the Ituri forest. The main groups are Mtubi, Aka, Baka, and Twa. Together they have a population between 130,000 and 170,000.

The Expert Says...

" Today … the Congo appears as the key to the economic development of the central African interior. "

— Roland Pourtier, professor of Geography, University of Paris

CRISIS IN THE CONGO

More people are moving into the Congo River Basin. Read these fact cards to learn more about how population growth is affecting the rain forest of the river basin and its environment.

Rain Forest

The population of the Democratic Republic of Congo is predicted to double to about 120 million by 2020. This is creating a demand for farmland. People are clearing the rain forest to plant crops. Once the land is no longer fertile, they move somewhere else, leaving the area barren and useless.

Wood Products

Timber demand from the rest of the world is becoming a serious threat to the rain forest. Countries like China, Europe, and the United States are importing large amounts of wood products. These are powerful reasons for the continued removal of trees.

Logging

An especially growing problem has been road building by logging companies. Roads provide transportation and easier access to the heart of the forests. This has resulted in the killing of animals such as the gorilla, elephant, and leopard by new poachers.

Environment

Today, environmental protection is at the top of the "to-do" list for many countries in the river basin. Wildlife and nature conservation are key issues. Better education and transportation, more jobs, improved public services, and more foreign funding and support are just a few of the many priorities. Environmental issues need to be well integrated into all of these efforts for positive changes to take effect.

? Research other rivers in this book with habitats that are in danger. Compare one of them with the Congo. How are they similar or different?

Although poaching of elephants for their ivory has declined since the 1989 ivory ban, it is still a widespread problem in west and central Africa.

Take Note

The Congo River takes the #4 spot. It is one of the largest rivers in the world, and the lifeblood of millions of people living in the river basin. The Congo and its tributaries provide an important waterway for transport across central Africa.
- How would you feel if your home were taken over by strangers? What do you think you could do to stop it?

5   **4**   3   2   1

The Yangtze River Valley supports over 350 million people. That's about one-third of China's population!

ER

LENGTH: Over 3,915 mi.

CONTINENT: Asia

WHY SO MIGHTY? The Yangtze has been an important part of China's history — it has been a source of water, food, and transportation for thousands of years.

To the people of China, the Yangtze is more than just a river. It is closely linked to the history of the country. In 2007, archeologists discovered human fossils dating back two million years in the Three Gorges area of the Yangtze River. Seven thousand years ago, people were fishing, planting, and building some of China's first settlements along the banks of the river. In the 20th century, Japanese soldiers traveled down the Yangtze during their invasion of China in World War II.

Other rivers may be longer than the Yangtze, but this waterway is special because it has about 350 million people living near it. For centuries people have been drawn to the Yangtze for trade, transport, and travel. It is honored for giving life to those who live along its banks. These people have farmed the nearby plains, fished in the deep waters, and traveled through the numerous tributaries. It is no wonder that the Yangtze is called "China's Lifeline."

In recent years, the Yangtze has come into the spotlight because of the Three Gorges Dam project. It will be the biggest hydroelectric project in the world, but the environmental impact will be far-reaching. Whatever the outcome, it is clear that this engineering project will change the face of our #3 pick and the lives of its people forever.

Gorges: *deep canyons*

YANGTZE RIVER

WHERE IN THE WORLD?

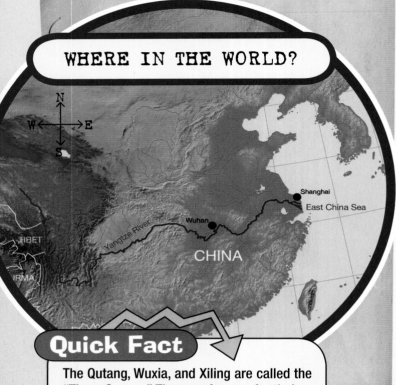

N
W — E
S

Shanghai
East China Sea
Yangtze River
Wuhan
CHINA
TIBET
IRMA

Quick Fact

The Qutang, Wuxia, and Xiling are called the "Three Gorges." They are famous for their height and beauty. At some points the walls of the gorges are as high as 2,950 ft.

This picture shows a tourist junk boat with large sails and bamboo masts. Traditionally, junk boats are used for transporting goods and people along the river. Some people even live in them!

MOMENT IN TIME

In the civil war of the 1940s, communist forces under their leader Mao Zedong made many strategic crossings of the Yangtze River and its tributaries. The communists drove the Nationalists from the mainland and formed the People's Republic of China in 1949. To prove his greatness, Mao Zedong swam across the Yangtze in 1956, 1958, and 1966. He even wrote a poem praising how people can control this great waterway.

LIFE ON THE RIVER

The crops of the Yangtze River Basin feed all of China. These crops include rice, wheat, corn, and cotton. Farming is made possible because of irrigation systems that have made agriculture very stable. Farmers and fishermen use sampans (flat-bottomed boats) and junks (boats with two to five masts) to move goods along the river. Larger ships can travel up to 430 miles inland to the city of Wuhan. These vessels carry food, manufactured goods, iron, steel, and oil.

Flooding along the river has been a major problem. Lives are lost and homes are destroyed. Damages from flooding are costly.

---

nationalists: *American-backed political party during World War II, now the governing party in Taiwan*

Quick Fact

The huge river system receives water from tributaries from the north and south of China. The flood season is from May to August. In the 20th century alone, there were five major floods killing over 300,000 people.

CHINA'S SECOND GREAT WALL

This article explains how the Three Gorges Dam will affect the Yangtze River and its people.

Once completed, the Three Gorges Dam will be the largest and most powerful hydroelectric project in the world. The dam will create a reservoir that's nearly 400 miles long, forever changing the landscape of this area.

The Three Gorges Dam is both a marvel and challenge of engineering. It has been designed to store over four trillion gallons of water and to withstand an earthquake of seven on the Richter scale. The reservoir will allow 10,000-ton freighters to enter the country's interior by deepening water levels so heavier boats can float through. It will also control floods and give electrical power to China's growing cities.

China's leaders believe the Three Gorges Dam represents progress and pushes the nation's economy into the 21st century. But it may also force over one million people to leave their homes, flood over 1,000 archeological sites, and cause some animal species to become extinct. Many people are worried about a buildup of sediment in the dam that could cause more floods. Toxins from sunken mines and factories could also leak into the reservoir water.

Like China's Great Wall, the Three Gorges Dam will be one of the few structures visible from space. The question is, do the pros outweigh the cons of this project?

---

reservoir: *human-made lake where water is stored for later use*
Richter scale: *system used to measure strength of an earthquake*
sediment: *material that settles at the bottom of a river*

The dam is more than 600 feet high and stretches almost 1.5 miles across.

The Expert Says...

" Continuing water shortages, which date from long before the drought, have had a drastic effect on fish resources in the Yangtze …

— Li Zhenye, director of marine farm administration in Tongling

Take Note

The Yangtze flows into the #3 spot. It is a lifeline for about 350 million people and has played an important role in shaping the history of China.
• Compare the Yangtze River to another river you have read about so far. Do you agree the Yangtze should rank #3? Why?

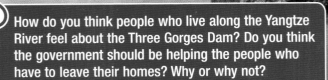

? How do you think people who live along the Yangtze River feel about the Three Gorges Dam? Do you think the government should be helping the people who have to leave their homes? Why or why not?

THREE GORGES DAM–GETTY IMAGES; ALL OTHER IMAGES–SHUTTERSTOCK.ISTOCKPHOTO

5   4   **3**   2   1

② NILE RIVER

The Nile River Delta is slowly being worn away by the waves of the Mediterranean Sea. Yearly flooding used to deposit new sand and silt into the delta, which would help build it back up. Now that the Aswan High Dam has been built, the flooding has stopped.

THE NILE RIVER—ISTOCKPHOTO

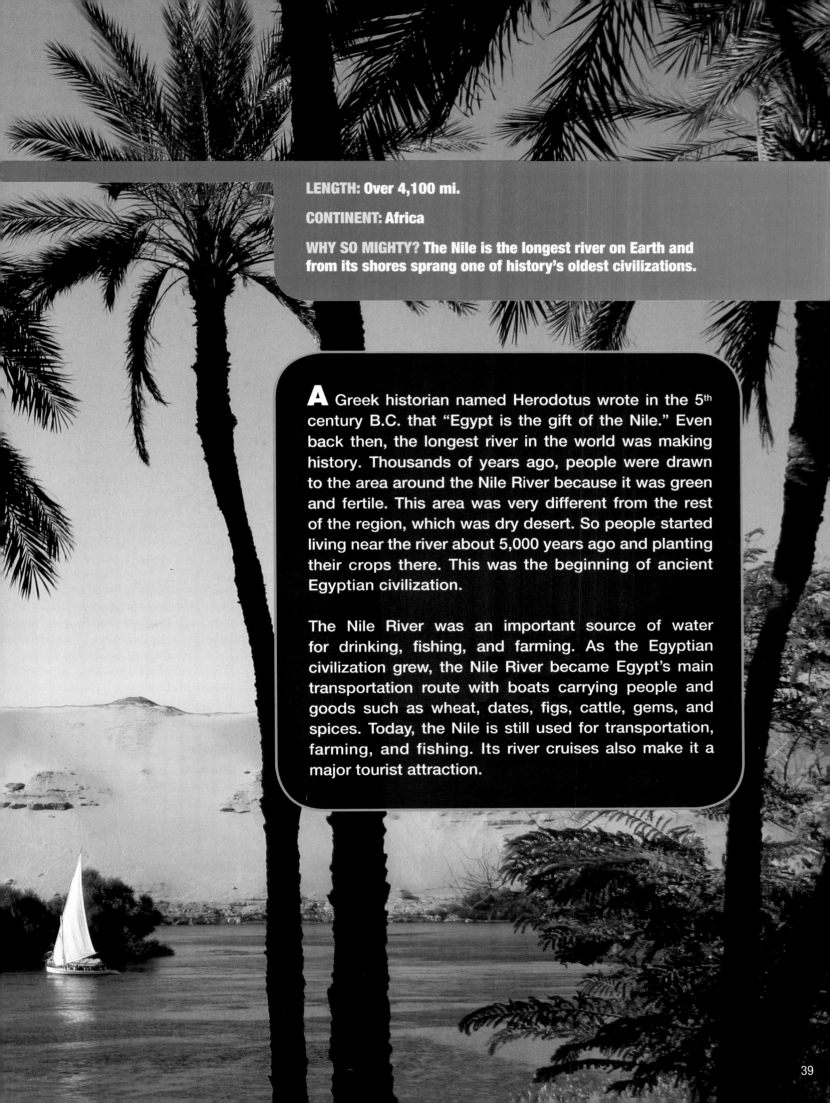

LENGTH: Over 4,100 mi.

CONTINENT: Africa

WHY SO MIGHTY? The Nile is the longest river on Earth and from its shores sprang one of history's oldest civilizations.

A Greek historian named Herodotus wrote in the 5th century B.C. that "Egypt is the gift of the Nile." Even back then, the longest river in the world was making history. Thousands of years ago, people were drawn to the area around the Nile River because it was green and fertile. This area was very different from the rest of the region, which was dry desert. So people started living near the river about 5,000 years ago and planting their crops there. This was the beginning of ancient Egyptian civilization.

The Nile River was an important source of water for drinking, fishing, and farming. As the Egyptian civilization grew, the Nile River became Egypt's main transportation route with boats carrying people and goods such as wheat, dates, figs, cattle, gems, and spices. Today, the Nile is still used for transportation, farming, and fishing. Its river cruises also make it a major tourist attraction.

NILE RIVER

WHERE IN THE WORLD?

Mediterranean Sea

N
W — E
S

EGYPT
LIBYA
Lake Nasser
JORDAN
SAUDI ARABIA
Nile River
Red Sea
CHAD
SUDAN
ERITREA
YEMEN
Gulf of Aden
SOMALIA
ETHIOPIA
CENTRAL AFRICA REPUBLIC
DEMOCRATIC REPUBLIC OF CONGO
UGANDA
KENYA
Indian Ocean

MOMENT IN TIME

In the early days, people who lived along the Nile River built homes from papyrus reeds tied together. The walls of their homes were made of straw, mud, and clay. Later settlers used the clay to build bricks. Small villages then started to appear. The people from these villages learned how to use the water during the seasonal floods. As time passed, they also became better farmers. Each year when the Nile flooded, it left a new layer of alluvium (fertile silt). This provided farmers with natural fertilizers for their crops.

Quick Fact

The Aswan High Dam was completed in 1970 to control the Nile's flooding. This dam created a huge artificial reservoir called Lake Nasser, forcing thousands of people to relocate. Farmers now have to use artificial fertilizers for their crops because natural fertilizers left behind by floods are no longer available for local farmers.

LIFE ON THE RIVER

The Nile River is Egypt's main water source. This is why most Egyptians live no farther than seven miles from its banks. The Nile River Basin covers an area of more than one million square miles where people grow crops such as cotton, corn, and sugarcane. The river also provides fish for food. The building of hydroelectric dams to provide power has brought about great changes to the land, endangering the ecosytem of the area.

papyrus: *water reed that grows along the banks of the Nile*

? Dams have been built across several of the rivers in this book. Would you like to live close to a dam? Why or why not?

Quick Fact

The Nile's natural wealth has attracted invaders from as far back as the 17th century B.C. These invaders included the Hyksos from Syria, the Persians, the Greeks, the Romans, the British, and the Germans.

Aswan High Dam in Egypt

Nile crocodile

7

6

EGYPT'S LIFELINE

This article explains why the Nile River was sacred to ancient Egyptians.

Ancient Egyptians depended on the Nile for their survival. It was so important that it affected the religious beliefs of the people. They prayed for its floodwaters and even created a god for the river named Osiris.

Belief in the afterlife was a major part of ancient Egyptian religion. The Nile played a role by symbolizing both life and the afterlife. Egyptians saw that the sun rose in the east and believed this symbolized birth, and set in the west, symbolizing death. Because of this, all ancient Egyptians were buried on the West Bank of the Nile, which symbolized the connection between life on Earth and the afterlife.

The Egyptians honored their dead, especially their pharaohs. This led to the building of giant pyramids, temples, and monuments in their honor.

Hieroglyphics and murals found in these structures tell us a great deal about Egyptian life. Tomb paintings illustrate how religion played an important role in shaping Egyptian society. Many believe the first written language developed from the need to keep records of death, flood, harvest, and rainfall.

Egypt became one of the most important civilizations of ancient times. The Nile River played a big part in helping the civilization to grow and develop.

hieroglyphics: *ancient system of writing using symbols and pictures*

Sobek — the Egyptian god symbolizing fertility — and the Nile River is often pictured as a man with the head of a crocodile.

? Compare the Nile and the Ganges. Why do you think these two rivers hold so much religious importance?

An ancient statue of Osiris, the river god

The Expert Says...

On the building of the Aswan High Dam:

" The sediment created a balance. Now the coastal processes are acting alone without sediments counteracting, and the balance has been changed. "

— Omram Frihy, retired coastal researcher in Alexandria

Take Note

The Nile may be the longest river in the world, but it still only ranks #2 on our list. Its mightiness comes from the fact that it was responsible for the development of the entire Egyptian civilization.

• At one point in ancient history, Egypt was one of the most powerful civilizations in the world. How do you think the Nile River helped to make this possible?

5   4   3   2   1

The Amazon River floods during the rainy season, which lasts from November to June. These floods are beneficial because they enrich the soil of the surrounding forests.

AMAZON RIVER—© LAYNE KENNEDY/CORBIS

VER

LENGTH: About 3,975 mi.

CONTINENT: South America

WHY SO MIGHTY? The Amazon carries the largest amount of water and supports the most diverse ecosystem on the planet!

The Amazon River is the most voluminous river on Earth. It holds 11 times more water than the Mississippi, it drains an area equal to the size of the United States, and it has a basin the size of Australia. During the high-water season, the river's mouth can be almost 300 miles wide and its daily fresh water release into the Atlantic Ocean is enough to supply New York City with water for nine years. The force of the river's current pushes water 125 miles out to sea before it mixes with Atlantic salt water. In the early days, European explorers could drink fresh water out of the ocean before sighting the South American continent.

Not only is the Amazon River gigantic, but it runs through the world's largest tropical rain forest. Inside the 2.4 million square miles of the Amazon Basin lies a wealth of life richer than anywhere else on the planet. On top of the many species of life-forms we know about, there are millions waiting to be discovered.

Uncontrolled deforestation and mining are threatening the future of this amazing habitat. If this damage continues, scientists estimate the Amazon could become a savanna by the year 2080. For many, the battle to save our #1 pick is front and center.

---

voluminous: *large in number or quantity*
savanna: *flat grassland dotted with trees*

AMAZON RIVER

WHERE IN THE WORLD?

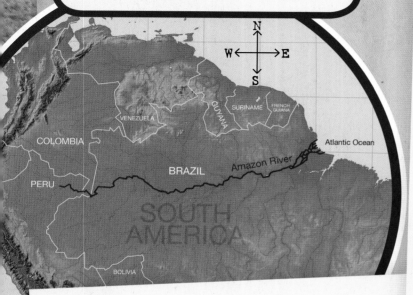

Quick Fact

The mouth of the Amazon is more than 245 miles wide. The flow measures about 6.6 trillion gallons a day, 60 times more than the Nile and 11 times more than the Mississippi.

LIFE ON THE RIVER

There are about 400 groups of indigenous peoples living in the area surrounding the Amazon River. Its rain forest is home to over 300 species of mammals, thousands of freshwater fish, tens of thousands of trees, and nearly 100,000 other types of plants. It is especially known for its many species of insects. Some experts believe there are close to 20,000, while others say the number is closer to a million. New species are still being discovered today! As the river with the most fresh water on Earth and running through the largest rain forest, the Amazon is very important to the world's environment.

indigenous: *native to the region*

MOMENT IN TIME

The first Europeans to discover the Amazon were Spanish explorers in 1542. They were led by Francisco de Orellana. They sailed from Peru to the Atlantic Ocean in search of gold and silver to bring back to their king. The first people they met in the rain forest were tall, female warriors. So Orellana named the river after a Greek myth about women warriors called "Amazons."

Why do you think it's important to study the many plants, animals, fish, and insects that grow and live in the Amazon Basin? How do you think this research could help people?

Quick Fact

Cattle farming was the cause of deforestation in the 1960s and 1970s. By the 1980s, the rate of destruction was overwhelming, with almost one-fifth of the rain forest cleared. Protecting the forest that is left is now a main concern.

Quick Fact

Native Amazonians have lived in the area for more than 20,000 years. When Europeans landed in the 16th century, the native peoples were scattered. As many as 90 percent of the inhabitants died within the first 100 years of contact because of European diseases.

The Expert Says...

" Deforestation is drying the planet, and the two factors that are driving the dehydration of [the Amazon Basin] are global warming and the removal of trees. "

— Eneas Salati, Brazilian physicist

dehydration: *extreme loss of water*

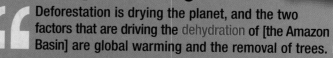

9   8   6

VANISHING ACT

Since the Amazon River Basin is so rich in natural resources, it has attracted many industries such as logging, ranching, mining, and tourism. At this point, 17 to 18 percent of the rain forest is gone. Many groups are working to protect this valuable environment before it is too late. This list counts down five reasons that make the Amazon rain forest unique.

1 The Amazon has the most diverse ecosystem on the entire planet with more mammals, fish, trees, plants, and insects than anywhere else in the world. One biologist even found more ants in one tree than in all of Great Britain! Many of its plants, animals, and insects could be wiped out before they are even identified.

2 Many medicines and drugs come from plants, fungi, and insects found in the rain forest. Deforestation may risk finding cures for deadly diseases. Perhaps the key to curing cancer might be found deep within the Amazon rain forest?

3 Have you taken a deep breath lately? Well, you can thank the Amazon's rain forest. It is described as the "lungs of the world." That's because it produces over 20 percent of the world's oxygen.

4 The Amazon's rain forest has a huge impact on the world's climate. As more trees are being cut, less rainfall is being created. Plus, with the destruction of the rain forest, global warming could get worse a lot faster, resulting in longer, more frequent droughts and melting ice caps.

5 The Amazon River contains more fresh water than any other river in the world. This is pretty amazing when you consider how little of the water on Earth is fresh and that most of it is frozen in glaciers.

? Why do you think that people all over the world, and not just Brazil, should be concerned about the destruction of the Amazon and its rain forest?

A section of dried riverbed along the Amazon in 2005. Scientists believe climate change has helped to cause the worst drought the basin has seen in 60 years.

Take Note

The mighty Amazon takes the #1 spot. This river not only affects its basin, but the entire world. It contains more fresh water than any other river in the world! Plus, it has the most diverse ecosystem on Earth, with millions of yet to be discovered plants, animals, fish, and insects!

• All but one river in this book is endangered. Research and report on one successful attempt to save a river.

2

1

We Thought …

Here are the criteria we used in ranking the 10 mightiest rivers.

The river:
- Is an important means of transportation
- Provides water for drinking and agriculture
- Has inspired great works of art, music, and writing
- Is large in length and volume
- Supports the economy
- Supports an impressive environment and wildlife
- Has shaped history
- Is a geographic landmark